Beggars of Life: A Companion to the 1928 Film

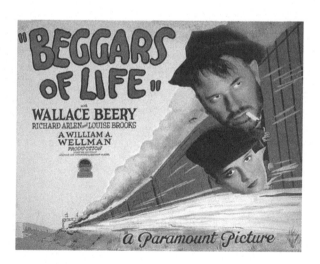

Beggars of Life: A Companion to the 1928 Film

Thomas Gladysz

Cover design by site bilder

A publication of the Louise Brooks Society
www.pandorasbox.com

All images from the collection of
Thomas Gladysz / Louise Brooks Society
except those otherwise credited

ISBN-10: 0-692-87953-6

ISBN-13: 978-0-692-87953-5

DEDICATION

To Christy Pascoe, my love and my companion
in my travels through the life and
legend of Louise Brooks

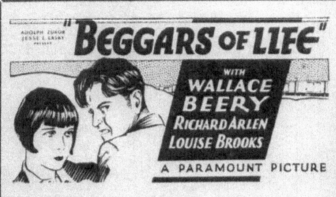

CONTENTS

ACKNOWLEDGMENTS

My sincere gratitude to Kevin Brownlow, Barry Paris, Christy Pascoe, Frank Thompson, and especially William Wellman, Jr., each of whom directly or indirectly contributed to this project. Thanks also to Paul Bauer, Mark Dawidziak, Amanda Howard, John Gallagher, Howard Prouty, Rodney Sauer, Philip Vorwald, and Bret Wood, as well as the following institutions and websites.

Discography of American Historical Recordings

George Eastman Museum

Kent State University Press

Louise Brooks Society

Academy of Motion Picture Arts and Sciences, Margaret Herrick Library

Media History Digital Library

Newspapers.com

San Francisco Public Library

San Francisco Silent Film Festival

Society for American Baseball Research

HE RULES A LAWLESS REALM

—a realm of seekers after dreams. Men who appear for a moment on the surface of life. Beg a crust of bread at the back door, a dime on the street. Then disappear. Where do they go? Why do they go? Wanderlust! A glimpse of the ways of the Wanderer by Jim Tully, the rover, the hobo, the tramp, risen to be one of America's best-known authors. Hobohemia as few people know it. The Wanderlust as few people experience it.

a Paramount Picture

"BEGGARS OF LIFE"

WITH
WALLACE BEERY
RICHARD ARLEN
LOUISE BROOKS

PRESENTED BY
ADOLPH ZUKOR
JESSE L. LASKY

FOREWORD

by William Wellman, Jr.

Thomas Gladysz has crafted an impressive and insightful chronicle as a companion piece to the 1928 film, *Beggars of Life*. He sketches a colorful portrait of this memorable black and white picture that my father, William A. Wellman, believed was the best of the twenty silents he directed.

In this statement, my Oscar-winning father is passing over not only his personal story, *The Legion of the Condemned*, but the prodigious *Wings*, winner of the first Academy Award for Best Picture and the *Star Wars* of its generation.

In a career of over 40 years, my father became one of the most versatile directors in cinema history. He directed 76 pictures of every type and scope with 32 Academy Award nominations and 7 Oscars. Time-honored films like *Public Enemy* (1931), *Wild Boys of the Road* (1933), *Heroes for Sale* (1933), *The Call of the Wild* (1935), *A Star is Born* (1937), *Nothing Sacred* (1937), *Beau Geste* (1939), *Roxie Hart* (1942), *The Ox-Bow Incident* (1943), *The Story of G.I. Joe* (1945), *Yellow Sky* (1948), *Battleground* (1949), *The High and the Mighty* (1954) among others.

On his favorite film list was always 1928's *Beggars of Life*. If anything, it climbed higher as his career continued forward. When he first read the script, it tapped into his visceral side bringing back memories of a turbulent childhood, problems with authority figures, a hunger for adventure.

My father filled the cast and crew of *Beggars* with people he had worked with and befriended. The few newcomers, like Wallace Beery, soon became friends—they teamed with 3 pictures. Richard Arlen, who became a star in *Wings*, did 5 films together. Sporting her signature short black hair and bangs in helmet style, Louise Brooks was another matter.

Director and star were hardly a match made in heaven. Wild Bill, my father's nickname, was highly enthusiastic and crazy about making movies in Hollywood. Lulu, on the other hand, was admittedly bored with films, doing the same thing over and over. She couldn't wait to get away from movies and Hollywood. When the two were assigned the same picture, trouble was a brewing.

But after filming commenced, the director and star began to appreciate each other's work. Wild Bill and Lulu never became soul mates. She was always trying to distance herself from the rest but did her work in a responsible way, even ready to perform her own stunts. There was a fighting spirit that seeped through and the director applauded that. He liked her independent nature, unafraid to speak her mind with total candor—as he always did.

My father wanted to work with her again, but after one more Paramount film, *The Canary Murder Case*, she left the country. Never out of my father's mind, he wanted her for one of his early sound films, *Night Nurse* (1931). It was rescheduled to follow the great gangster epic, *Public Enemy*. The director offered her the leading female role, the part eventually played by the Platinum Bombshell,

Jean Harlow. Brooks rejected the offer choosing to disappear to another town and another lover.

One of her biographers, Barry Paris wrote, "Turning down *Public Enemy* marked the real end of Louise Brooks's film career." If only she had listened to my father and done his enduring classic, her career would have been reinvigorated and her adoring fans would have had many more films to celebrate.

In Thomas Gladysz's rendition, we feel the love attached to this very special person with a hypnotically beautiful face, a subtle and captivating style, one of the first naturalistic actors in film and way ahead of her time.

About the picture, Oscar-winning writer and filmmaker, Kevin Brownlow wrote, "the rich, highly polished surface of technique gleamed through, revealing a style of astonishing elegance... brilliantly thought out and superbly made."

Beggars of Life is a true classic of silent cinema brought to light by the talent and passion of Thomas Gladysz.

* * *

William Wellman, Jr. is an actor and writer, and one of seven children born to director William A. Wellman and his fourth wife, actress Dorothy Coonan. He has numerous film and television credits to his name, including appearances in four of his father's films.

Wallace Beery was featured on the window card issued
by Paramount at the time of the film's release

INTRODUCTION

In 1928, thirty-two year old director William Wellman was at the top of his profession. He was still basking in the critical and commercial triumph of *Wings*—the first film to win the Academy Award for Best Picture—when his latest production, *Beggars of Life*, hit screens in the fall of that year.

Considered a Paramount "special" and the studio's most important dramatic production of the season, *Beggars of Life* was meant to provoke. The film's gritty realism—and its message of constant struggle—stood at odds with the otherwise carefree glitz and glamour of the Jazz Age.

The film was loosely based on a bestselling book[1] of the same name by Jim Tully, a celebrated, rough-and-tumble, two-fisted "tramp writer of Hobohemia" who established himself as the "Mighty Oak of Profane Letters." In Tully's book, a kind of novelistic memoir, the author gave a grim account of the nearly seven years he spent wandering America as a "road kid." It is a book not only about Tully's journeys (many of them made jumping trains), but also the colorful and sometimes unsavory characters he met along the way—in "hobo jungles," in jails, bars, and in small towns everywhere.

Though covered in a dusty realism, Wellman's movie

---

[1] Paramount also based the film on *Outside Looking In*, a stage play by Maxwell Anderson adapted from Tully's book.

tells a somewhat different story. *Beggars of Life* is a tersely filmed drama about an orphan girl (Louise Brooks) dressed as a boy who flees the law after killing her abusive stepfather. With the help of a young tramp (Richard Arlen), the two hop a freight train, ending up at a hobo camp ruled by Oklahoma Red (Wallace Beery). In this hobo underworld, with the police on their trail, danger is never far away.

Wellman's artfully photographed, morally dark tale of the disheveled and down-and-out stars Beery. He receives top billing, and gives a fine performance throughout the film. However, it is Brooks who dominates the screen in what is arguably her best role in her best American film.

Brooks stands out. And not just for her androgynous appeal. Rather, it is for her striking performance. Whether

Courtesy of William Wellman, Jr.

16

dressed as an at risk young woman or young man, Brooks seemingly reached down inside herself—perhaps for the first time in her career—and gave an emotionally riveting performance. She would do so the following year in *Pandora's Box* and *Diary of a Lost Girl*, two films where she once again plays a character who is sexually abused. How much Brooks' performance in *Beggars of Life* tapped into her own experience as a victim of sexual abuse we will never know, but, in all likelihood, it's there in ways the camera could not record.

Beggars of Life was released as both a silent and sound film (the latter with added music, sound effects, and dialogue) in September of 1928. The sound version played in larger markets, while the silent version played in smaller towns and those markets not yet "wired for sound." On a number of occasions, it preceded or

Courtesy of William Wellman, Jr.

followed or was paired with Wellman's still popular 1927 film, *Wings* (to which sound effects had also been added). Despite not being a full-fledged talkie, *Beggars of Life* enjoyed a long run and remained in circulation for nearly two years, as both sound films and the Depression overtook the country. One of the last American screenings took place in Phoenix, Arizona in early 1930.

After that, *Beggars of Life* fell into obscurity. In 1943, Deems Taylor gave the film a rare shout-out in his classic text, *A Pictorial History of the Movies*. In the chapter on the coming of sound, Taylor wrote "*Beggars of Life*, a screen version of Jim Tully's grim novel... differed from the average 'sync' picture in that it had several sequences of actual dialogue." That brief passage was the last anyone would hear of the film for some time.

In the early 1950s, *Beggars of Life* was saved from destruction by curator James Card, who began occasionally showing the film at the George Eastman House in Rochester, New York. It was there and then that the movie began its slow journey back.

Beggars of Life, along with Brooks herself, reemerged in the 1960s: in 1965, the film was screened at the National Film Theatre in London. And in 1968, the actress published "On Location with Billy Wellman," her vivid memories of working on the film. Both events stirred interest

Recently, the surviving 16mm print owned by the renamed George Eastman Museum was optically enlarged to 35mm, with the result being the movie is now increasingly shown at festivals and other special events around the world. In the United States, the Mont Alto Motion Picture Orchestra has accompanied the film on a number of occasions, playing an original score that is both nuanced and historically aware. And in England, the film has been screened with musical accompaniment by The Dodge Brothers, a raucous group who play a blend of American roots music and English skiffle. The group, which includes film critic Mark Kermode and occasionally silent film pianist Neil Brand, have accompanied *Beggars of Life* at all manner of venues, including the Royal Albert Hall and even the Glastonbury Music Festival.

In 2017, *Beggars of Life* enjoyed its first real commercial release when Kino Lorber issued the film on DVD/Blu-ray in the United States.

Beggars of Life is a small masterpiece, and in ways, it is a film ahead of its time. In the words of film historian Bryony Dixon, who included the movie in her book, *100 Silent Films* (British Film Institute, 2011), "… it is a film to wallow in—yes, it *is* unrealistic, and it *is* sentimental, but it is so charming and beautiful, and the characters so endearing, that we are all delighted to forgive it any such minor faults."

Courtesy of William Wellman, Jr.

Jim Tully (top, far right – bottom, far left) visits the shoot

JIM TULLY & BEGGARS OF LIFE

Jim Tully (1886-1947) was hard to miss, either in person or on the printed page. Charles Willeford, a writer of hardboiled detective fiction and one of Tully's literary heirs, described him as "a short stocky man, without much neck. His arms and shoulders were powerful, and he was physically strong from driving tent stakes, making chains, fighting, and hanging on to the iron ladders of fast intercontinental freights. His kinky red hair, too thick to be combed, resembled Elsa Lancaster's electrified hair in... *Bride of Frankenstein*."

Born in 1886 near St. Marys, Ohio to an Irish immigrant ditch-digger and his schoolteacher wife, Tully experienced what can only be described as an impoverished childhood. After his mother died in 1892, Tully's father was unable to care for his children, and the six year old Tully was sent to a Catholic orphanage in Cincinnati, where he received his only formal schooling. At age 12, Tully's father removed him from the orphanage and gave the boy to an abusive farmer who employed Tully as a laborer.

Around age 14, Tully ran away and returned to St. Marys, where he found work in a factory. Lured into life on the road by the down and out he met near the railroad yard, Tully ventured out on his own. From 1901 to 1907, he traveled the country as a "road kid." He spent most of his teenage years in the company of hoboes, drifting across the country, jumping trains, scrambling into boxcars, sleeping in hobo camps, begging meals at back doors, and walking the length of small towns, all the while trying to avoid railroad cops and local sheriffs. It was a hard, often dangerous life, especially for someone so young. Tully was twice jailed for vagrancy, and once almost died.

While not riding the rails, Tully spent time as a carnival worker, and learned to make chain in local factories. He also became a self-described "library bum," frequenting libraries in almost every town he passed through. Possessed by the dream of becoming a writer, Tully read what he found by the likes of Dickens, Dostoevsky, and Twain. Tully even stole library books, which he read on his many cross-country trips.

Weary of a vagabond existence after six years on the road, Tully jumped off a railroad car in Kent, Ohio. He had growing aspirations, and hoped to settle down to a more regular life. For the next few years, Tully worked on-and-off as a chain maker, professional boxer, newspaper reporter, and travelling tree surgeon. He made a small name for himself in the boxing ring, and once tended trees for future president Warren G. Harding. Tully also began to write, publishing occasional poems and articles in Ohio newspapers while working on what would become his first novel, *Emmett Lawler*.

Tully married, and in 1912, he and his family moved to California, where he found work as a tree surgeon while continuing to box. More importantly, he began writing in earnest, and once encountered his hero, Jack London.

After settling in Los Angeles, Tully also came to meet Hollywood luminaries like Lon Chaney, James Cruze, Eddie Sutherland, and Frank Capra. Another of his new friends was MGM producer Paul Bern, who invited Tully to a party knowing Charlie Chaplin would be there and that the former hobo and the Little Tramp would hit it off. They did. In 1923, Chaplin employed Tully as his publicist and ghost writer.

Around this time, Tully started work on his second book, *Beggars of Life*. Published in 1924 to great acclaim, the book gave Tully the means to leave Chaplin and turn his attention to what would become a steady stream of books and articles.

Tully used his new-found fame to launch a parallel career as a Hollywood journalist. Between 1924 and 1944, Tully contributed hundreds of articles on movie stars and directors and Hollywood goings-on to magazines and newspapers across the country. Whereas his friend Erich von Stroheim was known as the "man you love to hate" because of the villainous characters he played on-screen, Tully was known as the man Hollywood loved to hate because his frank profiles often offended his movie-land subjects. In an incident that has passed into legend, matinee idol John Gilbert, stung by what Tully had written in a *Vanity Fair* profile two years earlier, confronted the author at the Brown Derby restaurant. A fight ensued. Tully, an experienced brawler, threw a punch that knocked Gilbert out.[2]

Tully also wrote for serious magazines like *The Smart Set* and *American Mercury*, each of which was edited by his literary champion, H.L. Mencken. Tully followed the old adage, "write what you know," and he penned stories about his family and early life (*Emmett Lawler* and *Shanty Irish*), his time on the road (*Beggars of Life*), his days as a

---

[2] All would be forgiven: not long after their confrontation, Tully and Gilbert appeared together in the Wallace Beery film, *Way for a Sailor* (1930).

boxer (*The Bruiser*), working in a traveling circus (*Circus Parade*), Hollywood (*Jarnegan*), and the down and out (*Blood on the Moon* and *Laughter in Hell*).

Tully's writing about the outcasts of America—the hobos, ditch diggers, boxers, prostitutes, circus carnies and prisoners—earned good reviews. While some of his more sensational books ran afoul of the censors (notably *Ladies in the Parlor*), they also enjoyed commercial success and were praised by the likes of Langston Hughes and James M. Cain. Famed author Damon Runyon called Tully "unique... one of the finest living American writers." Rupert Hughes wrote that Tully had "fathered the school of hard-boiled writing so zealously cultivated by Ernest Hemingway," an assessment echoed by George Jean Nathan.

Tully's best known book, then and now, is *Beggars of Life*. It is also his finest work, the one where the author found his voice. *Beggars of Life* established Tully as a gritty chronicler of the American underclass. It also marked him, much to his chagrin, as a "hobo writer."

Originally titled *Tramp Days*, and subtitled by its publisher "A Hobo Autobiography," *Beggars of Life* was issued in August, 1924 by the prestigious New York publisher Albert & Charles Boni. The book sold well, and was widely reviewed. Though the *New York Tribune* and England's *Manchester Guardian* were critical, the *Los Angeles Times* praised it, as did most others. The *New York Times* said, "Jim Tully's book is autobiography naked and unashamed.... Nobody can read it and question its truth." The book also found fans in the film colony; among them were actors Raymond Griffith and Virginia Valli, each of whom commented in print about regarding their interest in the book.

Tully's book was a touchstone. In early 1925, Louise

Brooks was hired to play a small part in the Herbert Brenon film, *The Street of Forgotten Men*. Like *Beggars of Life*, it features a story set among the down and out. In its review of Brenon's film, the *New York Daily News* name-checked the hobo author, stating "*The Street of Forgotten Men* dips into the dark pools of life. It shows you the beggars of life—apologies to Jim Tully—and in showing them it shows them up." That same year, Maxwell Anderson, the future Pulitzer Prize winning dramatist, adapted *Beggars of Life* for the stage as *Outside Looking In*.

With Eugene O'Neill as one of three producers, *Outside Looking In* debuted September 7, 1925 at the Greenwich Village Theater. It received favorable reviews, along with near ecstatic praise from famed critic Alexander Woolcott. Besides its rough and tumble story, what impressed Woolcott as well as noted critic Burns Mantle was the acting, which everyone thought outstanding. Future screen great Charles Bickford played Oklahoma Red, bobbed Blyth Daly played The Girl, while newcomer James Cagney was cast as Little Red, a character based on Tully that became Arlen's The Boy.

Chaplin also praised *Outside Looking In*, calling it "one of the most powerful plays I have ever seen" in a letter to the New York *Herald Tribune*. At the time, the famous actor was in New York for the premiere of *The Gold Rush*.

During the summer of 1925, Chaplin and Louise Brooks met, and the two enjoyed a brief affair. One night, Chaplin decided he wanted to see the Tully play yet again—according to Brooks, it was for the third time—and the two lovers walked across town to the Greenwich Village Theater. Brooks was less impressed by the play: she later commented she would have paid more attention to its story had known she would one day act in the film.

Paramount's interest in *Beggars of Life* dates from this

time. A September 8, 1925 summary prepared for the studio stated "Play is very unusual and is highly entertaining. It depends greatly upon the dialogue and the unique characters... could be made interesting as a screen story."

The challenge to do so fell to another rough-and-tumble up-and-comer, William Wellman.

Jim Tully, ex-hobo "grown articulate," and Director William Wellman will collaborate on the filming of "Beggars of Life," the Tully novel just bought by Paramount. Tully is also the author of "Jarnegan," a story of a Hollywood director

Paramount purchased the rights to *Beggars of Life* in early 1928

William Wellman (top, far left – bottom, sitting on platform)
Courtesy of the Academy of Motion Picture Arts and Sciences
Margaret Herrick Library / William Wellman papers

WILLIAM WELLMAN AND
THE MAKING OF THE FILM

Throughout much of his career, William Wellman (1896-1975) was a contract director who alternated between stories assigned him by the studio and those he really wished to direct. *Beggars of Life* was among the latter. In fact, according to his son, Wellman thought *Beggars of Life* was his best silent film. In 1965, when the director was honored with a retrospective at the San Francisco International Film Festival, Wellman announced plans to bring Louise Brooks to the event and screen the then little seen movie. In the end, a print could not be obtained, and instead the Festival screened *Wings* at the local Masonic auditorium.

Wellman's rough-and-tumble manner earned him a large reputation; he was known for telling tales of his exploits as a flyer in the First World War, as well as for bullying actors to get the results he envisioned for the screen.

Wellman had his own troubled start in life. After the war, he worked his way up the Hollywood ladder after friend Douglas Fairbanks secured him a role in *The Knickerbocker Buckaroo* (1919). More comfortable behind the camera than in front, Wellman quit acting and soon found work behind the scenes. He made his directorial debut with a western, *The Man Who Won* (1923).

Wellman continued working in the same vein, directing Buck Jones' westerns and the occasional comedy until late 1926. Due in part to his reputation as a military hero, Paramount entrusted him with *Wings*, a major production set during the war. Praised for its realism and technical prowess, the aviation epic was enormously popular and critically acclaimed. It went on to win the Academy Award for Best Picture at the first annual Academy of Motion Picture Arts and Sciences ceremony in 1929.

A string of tough-minded movies followed, including *The Legion of the Condemned* (1928), *Beggars of Life* (1928), and *Chinatown Nights* (1929). In the 1930s, Wellman achieved popular and critical success with *The Public Enemy* (1931), *Night Nurse* (1931), *Nothing Sacred* (1937), the original *A Star Is Born* (1937), and *Beau Geste* (1939). He also made another terrific hobo-themed movie, *Wild Boys of the Road* (1933), casting future wife Dorothy Coonan as the cross-dressing female lead. Classics like *The Ox-Bow Incident* (1943) followed.

Beggars of Life is a Wellman film through and through. In it, he did what he did in all his films: he strove to improve the story as well as the look of the film by adding realistic detail, bits of humor, interesting visuals, and unusual camera angles and movement.

The film's company, numbering 75, nearly took over Jacumba, California—a hot, dry, resort town of 400 inhabitants located near the Mexican border. The movie's seventeen days of nearby outdoor location work were filled with not only hair-raising stunts, but also, undoubtedly—as there were very few women on location—carousing, drinking, rough housing and male camaraderie.[3] The extras, Brooks recalled in "On

---

[3] The few women present included Brooks, her Russian maid Anna, and Wellman's wife at the time, Margery Chapin, who served as "script girl," the film's uncredited script supervisor.

Location with Billy Wellman," were "twenty riotous hobos selected by Billy from among the outcasts who financed leisurely drunks by working as extras in films."

As some idled away the hours, Wellman was busy rehearsing and filming dangerous stunts on the trains. Since few trains ran on this stretch of track, Wellman had blocks of time to get things right, no matter the cost. In her essay on the film, Brooks recounts the story of how her male stunt double, Harvey Parry, was thought to have died after Wellman asked him to leap off a moving train to the rocky canyon below.

Wellman was determined to stage the film's action scenes as realistically as possible, and not resort to undercranking the camera, a trick used by filmmakers to create the illusion of speed. There was little Wellman would not try. Brooks remembered the train engineers were "dazed by the unconcern with which a runaway flatcar and the caboose were plunged into the gorge, taking with them the second camera and missing the second cameraman by inches."

Wellman was a demanding taskmaster. Brooks thought the director practiced a "quiet sadism" behind the camera. The cast and crew were alarmed when the director persuaded Brooks to take the place of her stunt double and hop a fast-moving boxcar, which nearly pulled the actress under its wheels.

As film historian Frank Thompson notes, *Beggars of Life* is a testament to the director's "exhilaration with movement. All of the characters are constantly in motion," either walking down the road or riding on trains, automobiles, or even a slow-moving bread-cart. Thompson also notes that at any given time, when Wellman wants to reveal something about a character, he shows us their feet. These symbols of motion were accompanied by the filming of motion. As in *Wings*—where a camera was strapped into an airplane, in *Beggars of Life* a camera was strapped to one boxcar while the actors played a scene on another and the train sped down the tracks.

According to the Wellman Jr. biography, *Beggars of Life* was "made as a silent, then Paramount, against the director's wishes, forced sound into it." A bit of dialogue (song lyrics actually) was first heard well into the movie, in the scene when Oklahoma Red (Beery) enters the story. Paramount executives wanted the stout actor to arrive, stand in the midst of the hobo camp, and sing a song. Wellman thought such a scene would prove static, and the director asked Beery to instead walk into the

Locomotive 102 and some of the cast and crew
Courtesy of the Academy of Motion Picture Arts and Sciences
Margaret Herrick Library / William Wellman papers

camp while singing and carrying a barrel of moonshine. The soundmen insisted it couldn't be done, and that the microphone couldn't be moved.

The director's near obsession with movement led to a solution, and something of an innovation. Others have been credited with first moving a microphone during the making of a film, but according to David O. Selznick (the brother of Myron Selznick, Wellman's agent), Wellman did it first for Paramount. Selznick made his claim to Kevin Brownlow, who included it in his 1968 book, *The Parade's Gone By*. "I was also present on the stage when a microphone was moved for the first time by Wellman, believe it or not. Sound was relatively new and at that time the sound engineer insisted that the microphone be

Richard Arlen, William Wellman, and Edgar Washington
Courtesy of the Academy of Motion Picture Arts and Sciences
Margaret Herrick Library / William Wellman papers

steady. Wellman, who had quite a temper in those days, got very angry, took the microphone himself, hung it on a boom, gave orders to record—and moved it."

During the making of *Beggars of Life*, numerous stories emerged in the press as to goings on behind the scenes. The Hollywood press was curious about the film, not only because it was thought an important production, but because of what was considered its novel theme and unusual location shoot.

Syndicated reports appeared in newspapers around the country. Some were little more than embellished studio publicity, though others had at least some basis in fact. A few stories concerned Tully (who visited the film on location) or Wellman (he reportedly bought a worn coat for the film from a real hobo he came across on Main Street), while others concerned the actors involved in the production (Arlen stopped shaving and was growing a beard).

At a time when some attended the movies to see their favorite stars dressed like millionaires, one story noted how inexpensive it was to dress actors as tramps and hoboes. However, it simply wasn't true. Paramount production records shows the studio spent $850.00 to dress Brooks in *Beggars of Life*. That amount was $100.00 more than the actress was earning per week under contract to Paramount.

Another far more likely story suggested the revelry at least some enjoyed: "The company filming Jim Tully's story, *Beggars of Life*, recently went on location at Jacumba, a little town near the Mexican border. Jacumba sleeps during the day but at night four of the more talented citizens gather to form an orchestra and there is a dance—held next door to the one hotel. Louise Brooks, trying to sleep after a hard day before the cameras, finally arose, slipped a coat on over pajamas, and went to the dance hall. 'How much do you make a night?' she inquired of the orchestra leader. 'Oh, about ten dollars,' he said. 'Here's fifteen,' said Miss Brooks, holding out the currency. 'I'm hiring you to not play any more tonight'."

A gathering of the cast and crew – Wellman stands in the middle

SCREEN SCRAPS

TONSORIALLY LACKING

With Wallace Beery and Richard Arlen both looking as though they had lost their razors and lacked the price of a shave, and with Beery, Arlen and Louise Brooks all clad in weather-worn tramp clothes, "Beggars of Life" was launch the Paramo

MAKE FILM NEAR BORDER

Seventy-five members of Paramount's "Beggars of Life" company have left Hollywood for Jacumba Hot Springs near the California-Mexico border. There railroad sequences for the Jim Tully story will be made. Wallace Beery, Richard Arlen and Louise Brooks head the "Beggars of Life" cast. William

FREIGHT WRECK PLANNED

There should be a big thrill for filmgoers in one of the scenes of the film version of Beggars of Life from Jim Tully's book, which is being made into a film.

Twelve old freight cars have been bought by the company. They will be hurled over a cliff for one scene in which a railroad wreck is to be shown. They will drop 300 feet, it is said.

There must be some truth in the saying about birds of a feather. It wasn't until work was well under way on "Beggars of Life" that members of the company of make-believe hoboes compared notes and found that in real life their director, William Wellman, had run away from home at the age of 16; that Jim Tully, author of the story, had run away from an Ohio farm at 14; that Louise Brooks, who plays the runaway heroine of the picture, had fled from her home town in Kansas at the age of 15 to learn stage dancing in New York; that Richard Arlen, another featured member of the cast, had run away at 17 to get a taste of the world war, and that Wallace Beery, chief vagabond of the picture, had left home at 16 to join a circus.

Beery As a Playboy.

Wallace Beery prepared for his latest role in "Beggars of Life" by a vacation at his cabin at Silver lake in the Sierras. Before going he served as king of the Fresno Raisin day fete. Returning from camp to the studio for once he deserted his newest love, the airplane, and drove back in his famous mud-spattered automobile.

* * *

Though Wallace Beery is the star of *Beggars of Life*,
Louise Brooks and Richard Arlen dominate the screen

A CAST OF CHARACTERS

One of the strengths of *Beggars of Life* is its cast of colorful and colorfully named characters. They include Wallace Beery as Oklahoma Red, Louise Brooks as The Girl (Nancy), Richard Arlen as The Boy (Jim), Robert Perry as The Arkansaw Snake, Roscoe Karns as Lame Hoppy, and Edgar "Blue" Washington as Black Mose. Also appearing in the film, mostly in uncredited roles, are Robert Brower as Blind Sims, Frank Brownlee as the Farmer, Jack Byron as a Hobo, Jacques (Jack) Chapin as Ukie, Andy Clark as Skelly, John Webb Dillion as a Hobo, Dan Dix as a Hobo[4], Mike Donlin as Bill, Budd Fine as a Hobo, George Kotsonaros as Baldy, Horace "Kewpie" Morgan as Skinny, Johnnie Morris as Rubin, Harvey Parry as a Hobo, Tom Watton as a New Hobo, and Guinn Williams as a Cart Driver.

Wallace Beery (1885–1949), who plays Oklahoma Red, appeared in some 250 movies during a 36-year career. Prior to *Beggars of Life*, Beery played opposite Brooks in *Now We're in the Air* (1927), a comedy set during the First World War.

In 1913, Beery moved to Chicago to work for the Essanay Studios, which cast him as Sweedie, a Swedish Maid, a masculine character in drag. In 1915, Beery starred with then wife Gloria Swanson in *Sweedie Goes to College*. Beery's other notable silent films include *The Last*

---

[4] Dix also helped as a cook. His wondrous meals are recounted in *Wild Bill Wellman: Hollywood Rebel*.

of the Mohicans (1920), *The Four Horsemen of the Apocalypse* (1921), *Robin Hood* (1922), *The Spanish Dancer* (1923), *The Lost World* (1925), *Old Ironsides* (1926), and *Casey at the Bat* (1927).

Beery achieved his greatest fame in the sound era, alternating between comedic and dramatic roles, though increasingly playing the heavy. In 1932, his contract with Metro-Goldwyn-Mayer stipulated that he be paid $1 more than any other contract player at the studio, making him their highest paid actor. Today, Beery is best known for his portrayal of Bill in *Min and Bill* (1930) opposite Marie Dressler, as well as for *The Big House* (1930), for which he was nominated for an Academy Award, and *The Champ* (1931), for which he won the Academy Award for Best Actor. Beery also starred in *Grand Hotel* (1932) and *Dinner at Eight* (1933), as Long John Silver in *Treasure Island* (1934), and as Pancho Villa in *Viva Villa!* (1934). Beery also appeared in Wellman's *This Man's Navy* (1945), and continued in films until his death four years later. He was the brother of actor Noah Beery Sr. (who appeared alongside Brooks in *Evening Clothes*), and uncle of actor Noah Beery Jr.

Louise Brooks (1906–1985), who plays The Girl (Nancy), was a film actress and dancer noted for her bobbed hair, a style she wore at the height of her career. Brooks appeared in 24 films between the years 1925 and 1938.

Today, Brooks is best known for the three films she made in Europe, *Pandora's Box* (*Die Büchse der Pandora*), *Diary of a Lost Girl* (*Tagebuch einer Verlorenen*), and *Prix de beauté*. They form a kind of trilogy. Both *Pandora's Box* (1929) and *Diary of a Lost Girl* (1929) were directed by G.W. Pabst, one of the leading German directors of the time; he, along with the acclaimed French director René

Clair, co-authored the story of *Prix de beauté* (1930), which was helmed by Italian Augusto Genini. *Prix de beauté* was one of the earliest French sound films.

Prior to her work in Europe, Brooks appeared in 14 American films, of which *Beggars of Life* and Howard Hawks' *A Girl in Every Port* (1928) are considered the best. Brooks made her screen debut in 1925, playing a moll in an uncredited role in Herbert Brenon's *The Street of Forgotten Men*. Under contract to Paramount, she was featured in a string of light comedies alongside major names like Adolphe Menjou and Dorothy MacKaill. Among her co-stars was W.C. Fields, who starred opposite Brooks in *It's the Old Army Game*, a film directed by the actress' future husband, Eddie Sutherland. Other notable surviving films include *The Show Off* (1926, with Ford Sterling), *Love 'Em and Leave 'Em* (1926, with Evelyn Brent), and *The Canary Murder Case* (1929, with William Powell).

Brooks' career during the sound era is undistinguished. Her talkies include *God's Gift to Women* (1931, directed by Michael Curtiz), and *Overland Stage Raiders* (1938, with John Wayne). She retired into obscurity after the latter. In 1982, Brooks published a bestselling memoir, *Lulu in Hollywood*.

Richard Arlen (1899–1976), who plays The Boy (Jim), was a film and television actor whose long career spanned the years 1921 to 1976. Prior to *Beggars of Life*, Arlen played opposite Brooks in *Rolled Stockings* (1927), a romantic drama starring Paramount's junior stars.

Arlen is best known for his featured role as a pilot in the Oscar-winning *Wings* (1927), which co-starred Clara Bow, Charles 'Buddy' Rogers, Gary Cooper, and Arlen's first wife, Jobyna Ralston. The film, a smash hit, was Arlen's breakout role. He also appeared in Wellman's

Ladies of the Mob (1928), and *The Man I Love* (1929). Other notable early films include *Manhattan Cocktail* (1928), *Dangerous Curves* (1929), Victor Fleming's *The Virginian* (1929), and *Alice in Wonderland* (1933).

In the 1930s, Arlen was cast in less prestigious productions including numerous Westerns and war films. In 1939, Universal teamed Arlen with Andy Devine in a series of 14 action-comedies known as "Aces of Action." In the 1950s and 1960s, Arlen was active in television, guest starring in series such as *Perry Mason, Playhouse 90,* and *The Loretta Young Show.* In 1968, he and Rogers played

An atmospheric portrait of Richard Arlen

42

themselves on *Petticoat Junction*. The episode, titled "Wings," referenced the 1927 movie.

Robert Perry (1878–1962), who plays The Arkansaw Snake, appeared in more than 190 films between 1912 and 1960. In the 1920s, he had small roles in the Rin Tin Tin feature *Jaws of Steel* (1927), *Lights of New York* (1928), *Me, Gangster* (1928), and *The Singing Fool* (1928); in the latter film, he played a doorman, a role he would return to time and again. *Beggars of Life* was the best role of his career.

Starting in the early 1930's, Perry appeared in mostly uncredited roles. His stern persona lead to numerous bit parts in gangster films, as well as nearly 20 parts as a referee in boxing scenes. Perry played a referee in *The Champ* (1931), with Wallace Beery, a doorman in *My Man Godfrey* (1936), a gangster in *Each Dawn I Die* (1939), an officer in *They Died with Their Boots On* (1941), and a ringside trainer in *The Quiet Man* (1952). His last role was as a courtroom reporter in *Inherit the Wind* (1960). A favorite of Wellman, he appeared in nine of the director's movies, *The Man I Love* (1929), *The Star Witness* (1931), *Night Nurse* (1931), *Heroes for Sale* (1933), *Call of the Wild* (1935), *A Star Is Born* (1937), *Nothing Sacred* (1937), *Beau Geste* (1939), and *Roxie Hart* (1942).

Roscoe Karns (1891–1970), who plays Lame Hoppy, was an actor who appeared in nearly 150 films between 1915 and 1964. He specialized in cynical, wise-cracking, and often tipsy characters; his rapid-fire delivery enlivened many comedies and crime dramas in the 1930s and 1940s.

Karns appeared in two Best Picture Academy Award winners, Wellman's *Wings* (1927), and Frank Capra's *It Happened One Night* (1934). The latter is arguably his best-

Robert Perry, Roscoe Karns, and Jack Chapin

known role: in the film, Karns plays an annoying bus passenger who tries to pick up Claudette Colbert. In other films, Karns played a friend of the hero, a wisecracking cab driver, or brash newspaper reporter, as he did in Howard Hawks' *His Girl Friday* (1940). His other notable films include Capra's *Dirigible* (1931), *Alice in Wonderland* (1933), *Twentieth Century* (1934), *They Drive by Night* (1940), and *Woman of the Year* (1942). From 1950 to 1954, Karns played the title role in the television series *Rocky King, Inside Detective*. His son, character actor Todd Karns, also appeared in the show. From 1959 to 1962, Karns was cast as Admiral Shafer in seventy-three episodes of the CBS series, *Hennesey*, with Jackie Cooper.

Edgar "Blue" Washington (1898–1970), who plays Black Mose, was an actor and one-time prizefighter and professional baseball player. Washington appeared in 74 films between 1919 and 1961. Like Robert Perry, Washington appeared mostly in bit parts throughout his career. And like Perry, *Beggars of Life* marked a high point. The nickname "Blue" came from director Frank Capra.

Harold Lloyd helped Washington break into acting, and this pioneering African-American actor appeared in the legendary comedian's *Haunted Spooks* (1920) and *Welcome Danger* (1929). Sporadic roles followed, as Washington appeared in films alongside early stars

Ricardo Cortez, William Haines, Richard Barthelmess, Ken Maynard, and Tim McCoy.

Wellman worked with Washington again in *The Light That Failed* (1939). The actor also appeared in a few films helmed by John Ford, including *The Whole Town's Talking* (1935) and *The Prisoner of Shark Island* (1936). Other notable movies in which Washington had a small part include King Vidor's all-black production, *Hallelujah* (1929), Mary Pickford's *Kiki* (1931), *King Kong* (1933), *Roman Scandals* (1933), *Annie Oakley* (1935), *The Plainsman* (1936), and *Gone with the Wind* (1939). He was in three installments in the Charlie Chan series, and appears as a comic sidekick in the John Wayne B-Western *Haunted Gold* (1933). Washington had small roles in *The Cohens and the Kellys in Africa* (1930), *Drums of the Congo* (1942), *Bomba, the Jungle Boy* (1949) and other lesser fair. Unfortunately, many of these parts traded on racial stereotypes. His last role, as a limping pool hall attendant, was in *The Hustler* (1961), with Paul Newman.

Among the uncredited, supporting players is **Guinn "Big Boy" Williams** (1899–1962), the bakery cart driver. He received his nickname from Will Rogers, with whom he appeared in 15 films starting in 1919. The year after *Beggars of Life*, Williams was featured in an important

Black Mose, played by Edgar Washington, carries an injured hobo

supporting role in Frank Borzage's *Lucky Star* (1929). After that, he mostly played the sidekick in westerns such as *Dodge City* (1939), *Santa Fe Trail* (1940), and later, *The Alamo* (1960). Williams also appeared in Wellman's *A Star Is Born* (1937), as the Posture Coach. He was married to three actresses: the first was Kathleen Collins, a silent era actress, and the second was Barbara Weeks, a B-movie actress. His last wife was character actress Dorothy Peterson, whom he met in the 1940s. Prior to meeting Peterson, Williams was engaged to Lupe Velez; she broke off their engagement at the home of Williams' good friend, Errol Flynn. (Velez reportedly broke a framed portrait of Williams over his head and then urinated on the picture.)

Horace "Kewpie" Morgan (1892–1956), who plays Skinny, was a silent era comedian who appeared in nearly

100 films from 1915 to 1936. He appeared in Mack Sennett comedies as well as Buster Keaton's *Three Ages* (1923) and *Sherlock Jr.* (1924), and later on he played Ole King Cole in Laurel and Hardy's *Babes in Toyland* (1934). In her essay, he was remembered by Brooks as a 400 pound hobo named "Tiny."

George Kotsonaros (1892–1933), who plays Baldy, was a Greek-born actor with a unique nose. His menacing looks gained him roles as a tough guy or prizefighter at a time when boxing movies were a flourishing subgenre. Two such films in which he had supporting roles were *The Body Punch* (1929) and William Wyler's *The Shakedown* (1929). He also appeared in the Rin Tin Tin feature *While London Sleeps* (1926), Alexander Korda's *The Private Life of Helen of Troy* (1927), and in Mauritz Stiller's final film, *Street of Sin* (1928).

Taking a break during filming: "Kewpie" Morgan is far left

Johnnie Morris (1887–1969), who plays the energetic Rubin, is best remembered for playing Lucifer Pappy Yokum in *Li'l Abner* (1940). He started in films in 1912, and played in mostly bit parts throughout his career including roles as a musician in *Innocents of Paris* (1929) and as a tradesman in *Barbary Coast* (1935). Like Kotsonaros, Morris had a small role in Mauritz Stiller's *Street of Sin* (1928).

Andy Clark (1903–1960), who plays Skelly, started out as a child actor in 1912 and appeared in numerous Edison shorts; he was featured in *Andy Gets a Job* (1913), *Andy Plays Hero* (1914), *Andy Has a Toothache* (1914), *Getting Andy's Goat* (1914), and others. He also had an uncredited role in *Wings* (1927).

Jack Chapin (1909–1945), who plays Ukie, was an actor and sometime assistant director who appeared in

Johnnie Morris stands to the left of Wallace Beery

mostly uncredited roles throughout his career. *Beggars of Life*, his first film, may well mark the high point of his time before the camera. Chapin's other credits include an uncredited reporter in *King Kong* (1933), an uncredited sentry in William Wellman's *Men with Wings* (1938), an uncredited fireman in Cecil B. Demille's *Union Pacific* (1939), and an uncredited photographer in *The Pride of the Yankees* (1942). The latter was one of a handful of sports-themed films in which he appeared.

Frank Brownlee (1874–1948), who plays the lecherous farmer, was a burly supporting actor often seen in gruff roles or as a heavy. He was a favorite of Hal Roach, who used him as a foil in Charley Chase's *Be Your Age* (1926) and the Laurel & Hardy comedy *Do Detectives Think?* (1927). Brownlee also had an uncredited part as the Mountain Girl's Brother in *Intolerance* (1916).

Frank Brownlee, center, played the lecherous farmer

24A—Background in blue, red and brown; title in white; star's name in orange; Paramount Picture line in orange; remainder of lettering blue................$2.40

JOY seekers on the highway are alive to entertainment possibilities. They are ready to grasp the first suggestion of a good time. They are coming in large numbers, in automobiles which make travel pleasant and entertainment available.

Posters are the guide posts. Joy seekers respond to them if they offer enjoyment. Eyes are continually on the lookout.

Are the guide posts these joy seekers see guide posts to your theatre? Are they Paramount Posters which promise "the best shown in town?" Are they Paramount Posters with your theatre name on them?

If not, why not? Joy seekers are seeking "The best show in town" and it's at your theatre when you play Paramount Pictures.

1A—Background in blue and maroon; star's name in orange; title in maroon; Paramount Picture line in orange; remainder of lettering in orange...........45

1B—Background in blue; title in white; Paramount Picture line in white; remainder of lettering in green...........45

POSTERS GUIDE THE SEEKERS

Build your own boards to cover locations which the regular boards in your town will not reach. The cost is negligible when the advertising return is measured. Get boards at unusual corners, on buildings, bridges, at turns in the road, in prominent downtown locations. Build boards and post posters for big results.

6A—Title in white; background in dark brown; Paramount Picture line in white; remainder of lettering in green...........50

3A—Background in grey blue; title in orange with white outline; Paramount Picture line in white; remainder of lettering in white.....45

3B—Upper background in green; lower background in black; title in white, with black shadow; Paramount Picture line in yellow; remainder of lettering in blue and white.....45

50

YOUR AUTOMOBILE CAN PAY DIVIDENDS

STOP grumbling at your garage bills. Make the bills boost your business. There is a thousand dollars worth of business wrapped up in every bill from your garage if you utilize the advertising power in Paramount's Cloth Banners. Make them pay your garage bill. Place them on your automobile and the automobiles of your employes and friends. The extra patronage they will bring will net you a neat profit. The original cost of the banners and the frames is negligible.

3' X 10'

BUILD auto banner frames for the running boards of your car and those of your employes and friends. They are cheap to construct and very effective. These frames should be 3' x 10', made of 1" x 2" stock. Bolt the frame to the running board of the car. When these frames are not being used on the cars they may be spotted around town. The colors of the banner on "Beggars of Life" are: Background in green; title in blue with white outline; Paramount Picture line in white; remainder of lettering in blue.

EACH $2

PARAMOUNT CLOTH BANNERS

COLORFUL DISPLAYS SELL PICTURES

EACH .... .87
GOLD FRAME .... .75

COLORS: Background in light blue; title in white; star's name in orange; remainder of lettering in blue.

THIS handsome drawing is an asset to any window. Don't forget to use it in all your displays, in the window displays of your best stores; in prominent downtown locations. It is artistic; it has selling power.

THE WINDOW CARD

PER M............$3.50

COLORS: Red and black.

GET your large department stores to include a Herald on "Beggars of Life" in each package leaving the store. Get them to the homes of prospective patrons. Distribute them on your mailing list.

THE HERALD

Louise Brooks - femininity and androgyny

WHAT THE CRITICS SAID

In 1928, there were great expectations about *Beggars of Life*. Not only was the film based on a bestselling book by a celebrated author, but just as importantly, it featured three major stars and was helmed by the man who only the year before directed one of the biggest films of the time. By such reckoning, *Beggars of Life* should have been a sensation.

In all likelihood, what kept it from widespread popularity was its grim story, one at odds with the upbeat tenor of the times. (The stock market crash and subsequent Depression were still a year away.) One Baltimore newspaper quipped about what it saw as the film's limited appeal: "Tully tale not a flapper fetcher for the daytime trade."

Not surprisingly, more than a few exhibitors were uncomfortable with its downbeat theme. The manager of the Garden theatre in Canton, Illinois critiqued the movie, saying it "Appealed to a few of the men, but not a thing pretty about the picture, and the women never cared for it." That comment was echoed by the manager of the Pearl theatre in Youngwood, Pennsylvania who described it as the "Wrong kind of picture for [the] American public. Enough bums of pictures, let alone 'Bum' pictures…. People kick on this kind." The manager of the Selma theatre in Selma, California went so far as to call the film "sordid and very vulgar."

The *Los Angeles Evening Herald* was similarly unsettled.

Though admitting the film was a "departure from the wishy-washy romance and the fervid triangle drama," the paper stated, "Considered from a moral standpoint, *Beggars of Life* is questionable, for it throws the glamour of adventure over tramp life and is occupied with building sympathy for an escaping murderess."

For *Educational Screen*, it was all too much. "So far as the ordinary observer is qualified to judge, the hobo part of the story is authentic. It is in the other aspects of his plot that the robust Mr. Tully runs a little awry. His casual young murderess and the circumstances surrounding the murder are outside the range of the probable, as anyone who reads the papers could tell Mr. Tully."

While some complained, others appreciated the film, while a few publications thought it had "unusual interest." The *Brooklyn Daily Times* considered it a "different sort of motion picture that comes as a real relief among offerings that are handicapped by sameness." The *San Diego Sun*

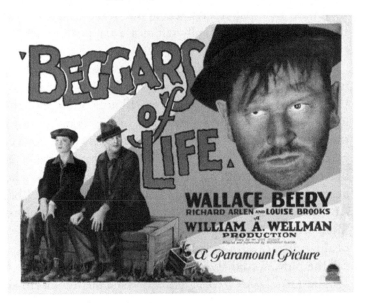

called it "strong stuff," while the *Cleveland Plain Dealer* described it as a "raw, sometimes bleeding slice of life." The *San Francisco Bulletin* touted the film's realism, while *TIME* magazine stated, "Here is a realistic reel."

For some publications, the film's grit was what made it worth seeing. The *San Diego Union* stated, "The picture provides an hour and a half of film entertainment radically out of line with the general run of cinema drama. It is pungent, powerful, appealing, masterfully directed and superbly acted." *Motion Picture News* noted, "It took a robust, morbid story to bring Wallace Beery back into his glory after floundering around for a season or two in half-baked comedy." Wellman's film, the journal also noted, "Has an earthy odor about it—and swings along with he-mannish strides. It spins its yarn with good gusto…. The picture has depth of plot, well defined characterizations and is interesting despite its heavy tread."

Wellman's direction came in for special praise. *Film*

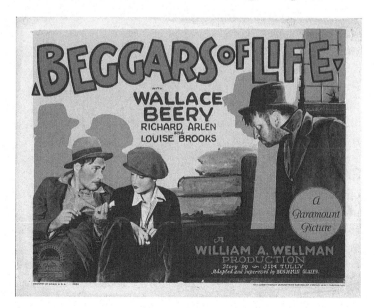

Spectator penned two appreciative reviews, one of which singled out the film's dramatic opening. "Another good bit was a scene where Louise Brooks describes a murder. It is much the same way in which Victor Seastrom showed thoughts in *Masks of the Devil*. Miss Brooks' face was superimposed upon the action which took place during the murder, and thus the audience got her reaction to everything. It was very interesting."

Also receiving praise were the core actors. Beery, the film's star, received his share, as did Robert Perry, who played in support but made a strong impression. So did Edgar Washington. *The Afro-American* newspaper wrote, "In *Beggars of Life*, Edgar Blue Washington, race star, was signed by Paramount for what is regarded as the most important Negro screen role of the year, that of Big Mose. The part is that of a sympathetic character, hardly less important to the epic of tramp life than those of Wallace Beery, Louise Brooks and Richard Arlen, who head the cast."

IT'S A GIRL!

LOUISE BROOKS IN THE PARAMOUNT PICTURE "BEGGARS OF LIFE"

Publications like the *Los Angeles Times* singled out the two actors at the heart of the story. "Richard Arlen and

Louise Brooks also capture honors for their sincerity and a poignant, moving quality they infuse into their roles without seeming to act at all."

With both the public and critics divided on particular aspects of the film, some focused on Brooks' unconventional role—one that played against type. Some publications liked the switch. *Motion Picture* declared "Louise Brooks is cute in her little trousers." Others, however, were not so appreciative. Louella Parsons, writing in the *Los Angeles Examiner*, commented, "I was a little disappointed in Louise Brooks. She is so much more the modern flapper type, the Ziegfeld Follies girl, who wears clothes and is always gay and flippant. This girl is somber, worried to distraction and in no comedy mood. Miss Brooks is infinitely better when she has her lighter moments." The *Detroit News* was only a little less disappointed, "Louise Brooks, who always looks gorgeous in beautiful clothes, suffers a bit from the man's garments called for by the role, but she does well."

The New York *Morning Telegraph* took a more nuanced view, "Louise Brooks, in a complete departure from the pert flapper that it has been her wont to portray, here definitely places herself on the map as a fine actress. Her characterizations, drawn with the utmost simplicity, is genuinely affecting." Another New York paper, *The World*, thought so as well, "Here we have Louise Brooks, that handsome brunette, playing the part of a fugitive from justice, and playing as if she meant it, and with a certain impressive authority and manner. This is the best acting this remarkable young woman has done." Even curmudgeonly Mordaunt Hall of the *New York Times*, long a critic of the actress, agreed, "Miss Brooks really acts well, better than she has in most of her other pictures." The *Pittsburgh Post Gazette* reflected a consensus, "Louise

Criticism pro and con ...

"If you have the tendency to be the least bit morbid, don't see *Beggars of Life* ... It is a depressing picture with nary a ray of light. But then, there are those who have a penchant for sadness ... Sordid and lurid." — *Milwaukee Sentinel*

"*Beggars of Life* was recognized as one of Paramount's major productions of the year, even aside from the sound feature. With the sound feature, it is overwhelming in its power." — *Hollywood Filmograph*

"The film, though interesting, does not exactly 'click.' Its virtue lies chiefly in providing Wallace Beery a chance to return to a heavy dramatic role, Louise Brooks to wear masculine clothes, and Richard Arlen to subordinate his looks to his acting. The film is essentially sordid." — *Evening Star* (Washington D.C.)

"Richard Arlen's juvenile vagrant, so delightfully played on the stage by James Cagney, is an excellent piece of work, while Louise Brooks's delineation of the girl fugitive is so good as to indicate that Miss Brooks is a real actress, as well as an alluring personality." — NY *Herald Tribune*

"... weakened by a conventional plot, a plot for which I see no reason except that it gives Louise Brooks a chance to wear boy's clothes and to jump a freight, both of which she always does, however, with an imperturbable maidenliness, generally to the synchronized accompaniment of sentimental music." — *New Yorker*

"Few pictures can boast of greater realism." — *Harrison's Reports*

"They've taken these hard-hearted hoydens of the highways and affixed little white wings to their shoulders, placed shining, incongruous haloes about their itching heads and put hearts of gold beneath their tobacco-stained vests." — *Ohio State Journal*

Brooks is interesting, with a cold, half-insolent beauty of face and figure masking a hidden fire. It is a new Louise Brooks."

All-in-all, *Beggars of Life* gathered its share of both criticism and acclaim, though most applauded the film. The *Chicago Tribune* named it one of the six best films for October, while the *Musical Courier* said it was "one of the most entertaining films of the littered season." *Film Mercury* deemed it among the year's better releases. So did *Film Daily* and *Weekly Film Review*.

Screenland summed up the opinion of many: "It's different. Instead of the dainty trippings of debutantes or the measured tread of marching men, or the clump clump clump of comedy villains, you have the tramping feet of the begging brotherhood … *Beggars of Life* is *The Big Parade* of the Hoboes. It reveals the private life of the knights of the road from haystack to box car, and it maintains its originality until the very end … Wellman also directed *Wings*. It seems to me his latest soars much higher than the aviation specials."

A publicity portrait of Louise Brooks

LOUISE BROOKS LOOKS BACK

Later in life, Louise Brooks looked back at her time in the movies. In letters to film historian Kevin Brownlow, and in the autobiographical essays collected in her book, *Lulu in Hollywood*, the actress recalled the films, directors, and actors which meant the most to her. In "The Other Face of W.C. Fields," she wrote about the comedian who starred in their 1926 film, *It's the Old Army Game*. And most significantly, in "Pabst and Lulu," she turned her attention to the German director and 1929 film for which she is best known today, *Pandora's Box*.

Another of Brooks' other films would also come under scrutiny. In 1968, the long retired actress published "On Location with Billy Wellman," her reminisces of the making of *Beggars of Life*.[5] In this 14 page autobiographical essay, Brooks focused largely on her working relationship with Wellman, as well as her personal, sometimes intimate, relationships with other members of the cast and crew. It was her most frank pieces of writing.

Brooks felt the director she worked with in her prior

---

[5] "On Location with Billy Wellman" first appeared in French translation in *Positif* (March 1968), and then in its original English in *London Magazine* (May 1968). Variants of the English version later collected in *Lulu in Hollywood* (1982) were also published in *Film Culture* (Spring 1972) and *Focus on Film* (Winter 1972), and excerpted in the anthology, *Voices of Film Experience: 1894 to the Present*, edited by Jay Leyda (1977).

film, Howard Hawks in *A Girl in Every Port*, had liked and even admired her. But with Wellman, it wasn't so.

Wellman and Brooks first met when she and Arlen were tested for their roles, and Brooks thought the director greeted her with suspicion rather than cordiality. In "On Location with Billy Wellman," Brooks wrote that even before they met, "Billy Wellman came to the unfortunate conclusion that since I did not follow the pattern of the actors who haunted the studio panting after film roles, I did not care about making films…. a coldness was set up between us which neither of us could dispel. Nor did hard work on my part and a willingness to do dangerous stunts under his direction alter Billy's conclusion."[6]

Brooks likely felt ill at ease. She just recently divorced from Eddie Sutherland, and, she was the one of the very few women on location. An account suggestive of her state of mind is found in Wellman's unpublished 1974 memoir, *Growing Old Disgracefully*, which is quoted in his son's biography. "I was bivouacked between two of the actresses, one of whom slept like a baby, the other [Louise Brooks] talked in her sleep, in intervals of the most interesting truths of different people… mostly men, and one important director [Eddie Sutherland] whom she had recently divorced that I knew very well, at least I thought I did, but after a week of listening to her, I knew him much better than even his mother. It was all very

---

[6] The coldness remained, but didn't keep Wellman from wishing to work with Brooks. In 1931, he offered her a part in *The Public Enemy*; Brooks turned down the role, and it went to Jean Harlow. A year later, when they met for what would be the last time, Wellman asked Brooks why she hated making pictures.

racy and entertaining, but unfortunately I started to dislike her, she was so different when awake, so sweet and lovely, and such a bastard when asleep and the truth came mumbling out."

Benjamin Glazer, who wrote the screenplay and supervised the film (and had a hand in adding sound effects), also came under Brooks' glare. The actress wrote Wellman directed the opening sequence of *Beggars of Life* with a "sure, dramatic swiftness that the rest of the film lacked." However, Brooks' thought Glazer's "artistic conception" of the film nearly destroyed what followed. After the opening scene, according to Brooks, the film's action grew slower. Only Wallace Beery's entrance saved it from the consequences of Glazer's "cultured supervision." The actress even thought Wellman too often waited on Glazer's approval when shooting a scene.

Brooks' scorn included herself, and she thought her own performance in the film an embarrassment. Brooks also disliked her co-star, Richard Arlen. They were friendly, but not fond of one another. "… his winning smile concealed a strong dislike for me," Brooks wrote, because "when we worked together in 1927 on *Rolled Stockings*, his vanity had made him quickly aware that I did not admire his acting."

One night, in the hotel lobby, Brooks and Arlen shared a bottle of whisky. They talked about Wellman and his war experiences, and their own lives. Arlen told Brooks he too had flown during the war. Brooks laughed at him in disbelief, and Arlen told her off. He went on a tear, criticized her acting, her looks, and the fact that her eyes were too close together. He criticized the fact she was paid more than he was, and the fact she owned a Lincoln town car. He also criticized her for divorcing Sutherland—who he considered a "swell guy."

Brooks had negative things to say about others involved with the film, including Tully. According to Bauer and Dawidziak's biography of the author, in May of 1928, prior to the company going on location, Tully wrote Mencken that he knew Brooks was "going around on the set calling me after Quilp—'unloved and unlovable'."

Decades later, she repeated her reference to the hunch-backed villain of Dickens novel *The Old Curiosity Shop*. According to the Barry Paris biography of the actress, Brooks wrote film historian Kevin Brownlow in 1967 that Tully "was the most repulsive little Quilp I ever knew," with "his belly hanging over his belt, yellow teeth to match his face and hair, full of the vanity of *Vanity Fair* and H.L. Mencken." Why she had it in for Tully isn't known. Perhaps it was because Brooks had heard her Hollywood friends express their hatred of Tully; or

perhaps it was because Brooks knew the author and her recently divorced husband were long time friends and drinking buddies.

In early June, Tully visited Jacumba to watch the filming of his book. (There were reports at the time that he would also appear before the camera, but apparently never did.) In a 1967 letter to Brownlow (quoted in the Paris biography), Brooks wrote "we were sitting on a rock posing for still pictures and he reached over and touched my breast, under a grey flannel shirt." It is a curious anecdote. Brooks allowed many to touch her, but, she always chose who. Tully was not among them.

Harvey Parry was. The daredevil stuntman had caught Brooks' eye when he doubled for Brooks and was almost killed jumping off a moving train. She had observed him around Jacumba, and though she loathed his character, she admired his powerfully trained body. One night, when the cast and crew was returning to town, she offered to leave her window unlocked, should he wish to visit. He did. The next morning, Parry loudly and in front of others asked Brooks if she had syphilis. To those gathered, the implication of Parry's question was clear. Humiliated, Brooks fled to her room.

Despite her many criticisms, Brooks didn't dislike everyone. She came to admire Wellman, as a director. And, she was fond of Wellman's 17-year old brother-in-law, Jack Chapin, who had a bit part in the film as well as a crush on the 21-year old Brooks. They hung around the town pool in Jacumba.

Surprisingly, Brooks also liked Wallace Beery. The two had worked together the previous year in *Now We're in the Air*, a comedy set during the First World War. The actor drove Brooks to Jacumba in his own car, and they talked about working in Hollywood and what to expect working under Wellman. Brooks was tense at first, but came to appreciate the sometimes brusque actor. In the end, she thought Beery saved the film, and considered his role as Oklahoma Red a "little masterpiece."

A portrait of Louise Brooks taken during the making of *Beggars of Life*

A surprising rapport also developed between Brooks and actor Robert Perry. As she revealed in a letter to Brownlow years later, the two became almost friendly, bonding over mutual feelings of low self-esteem drowned in whiskey.

In 1966, Brooks wrote to Brownlow, "Making the picture, I told Perry he was gorgeous and a great actor— (why didn't I go to bed with him instead of that smelly little double?)—and why didn't he take his career seriously? We were sitting 'round the fire in the jungle drinking whisky out of tin cups, at night, while Beery was working up on the ridge. Perry looked at his tin cup and said, 'This is what I work for—booze. You can't seem to understand—I'm a bum!' Later in the caboose, he was to even the score when he told me that I was an actress who had made a bum out of myself by screwing Harvey."

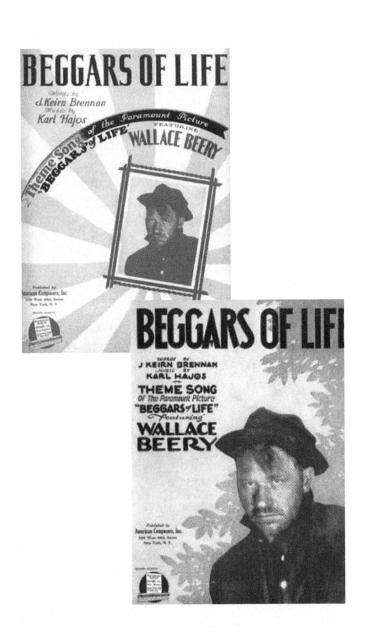

Two examples of film sheet music

SOUNDS OF MUSIC

The late 1920's marked a period of transition in the film industry, as both studios and exhibitors came to grips with emerging sound technologies. Hedging their bet, the major studios began releasing two versions of most every film, a sound version (often showcasing the latest technical advances), and a silent version meant to play in theaters not yet equipped to project sound.[7]

That was the case with *Beggars of Life*. At the time, sound was new, almost experimental, and Wellman was resistant to using it. According to film historian Frank Thompson, the director "felt that the intrusion of sound into his carefully constructed drama would be out of place and prove disturbing to the audiences and the mood." Wellman, however, was overruled, and Paramount General Manager B.P. Schulberg instructed special effect engineer Roy Pomeroy (who had served as a technical director on *Wings*) to supervise a scene that would feature a song sung by Wallace Beery.

Eventually, it was decided *Beggars of Life* would be released as both a silent and sound film. The sound version—recorded using the Movietone process—included sound effects, a synchronized musical score, a

---

[7] The theaters that received the silent version would have also received or purchased from their local exchange a cue sheet of musical themes for use by a local musician.

bit of dialogue, and a song. Though a few earlier Paramount releases had also utilized music and sound effects, *Beggars of Life* was, notably, the first studio release to include spoken dialogue.

The studio Press Sheet, headlined "Also Available with Sound," stated "For those theatres equipped to use Paramount's Sound Features, *Beggars of Life* has been prepared with Sound. Excellent music and effects are included in the synchronized score and *Beggars of Life* will take its place with those other masterpieces of Paramount screendom which, with Paramount Quality

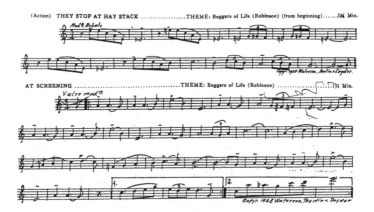

Paramount issued cue sheets, with suggested musical phrasing, for use by local musicians

synchronization, are making new motion picture history."

Though the film's sound elements are considered lost,[8] studio records, production records, newspaper articles, and even advertisements suggest what *Beggars of Life* might have sounded like.

Commenting on its New York City premiere, *Women's Wear Daily* noted, "Wallace Beery talks in this picture, sings a hobo song and ends with an observation about jungle rats in general." (According to the *New York Times*, Beery was heard referring to his hobo companions as "jungle buzzards.") *The World*, another New York paper, stated "there is a certain amount of 'sound,' such as the noise of the passing locomotive and the knocking at the door, employed, and for the first time movie patrons are permitted to hear the voice of Mr. Beery when he sings the chorus of a marching song." The *New Yorker* noted "the synchronized accompaniment of sentimental music."

At the time, sound was still novel, enough so critics around the country felt it necessary to comment on its use. The *Wisconsin News* wrote "By the way it is a sound picture and Wallace Beery speaks a few lines and sings a song. His speaking voice is splendid." The *Cincinnati Post* thought "Vitaphonic sounds" lent "extra force" to the film, an opinion shared by the *Los Angeles Times*, who wrote "Sound effects add to the story to a considerable degree. This is particularly true in the case of the runaway train." The *Boston Herald* noted "Most of the action is in or on freight trains. We see and hear them cutting through tunnels, rumbling along open spaces...." The *New Orleans Item* observed, "Vitaphone helps the story

---

[8] A Vitaphone disk for reel 1 is believed to have survived in the hands of a private collector.

This ad boasts "Completely synchronized *with* sound!

along with music that is fitting and well arranged. The 'Hallelujah I'm a Bum' rhythm helps the story's speed."

The response from trade and fan publications was similarly positive. *Picture-Play*, which once described sound film as "screechies," thought the sound effects in *Beggars of Life* added to, rather than detracted, from the film.

Where the sound version of the film was shown, newspaper advertisements often proclaimed something along the lines of "Come hear Wallace Beery sing!" But what that song was (and whether the whisky voiced actor actually sung it) is far from certain.

A few newspaper advertisements for the film, including the New York City ads for the premiere, mention the songs "I Wonder Where She Sits at Night" and "Beggars of Life." Other sources, including the director's son, site two similar titles, "Hark the Bells" or "Don't You Hear Them Bells?"

"Beggars of Life" (penned by composer Karl Hajos and lyricist J. Keirn Brennan) was considered the film's theme song.[9] The label on the Victor 78rpm recording affirms as much, noting it is the "Theme Song of the Motion Picture production *Beggars of Life*." According to surviving records, this version—an instrumental with vocal refrain, was recorded by The Troubadours[10] on September 13, 1928, about a week before the release of the sound version and almost two weeks after the silent version of the film began showing in the United States.

Around the time of the film's release, other recordings of "Beggars of Life" were released. Besides the Troubadours, there were recordings by the Bar Harbor Society Orchestra (featuring Irving Kaufman), as well as vocalists Scrappy Lambert, Seger Ellis, and others. The theme song proved popular, enough so two different editions of sheet music were issued. There was also a piano roll issued featuring a performance by Harold Wansborough.

A few additional clues as to the nature of the sound version of *Beggars of Life* can be found in the surviving records of an East Coast recording studio used by Paramount. According to the Discography of American

---

[9] On at least one occasion, the theme song was sung live before the film was shown.

[10] The Troubadours were a studio group directed by composer Nathaniel Shilkret. The instrumentation on this recording was listed as 4 violins, cello, bass, 4 saxophones, 2 cornets, 2 trombones, tuba, banjo, 2 pianos, and 2 traps.

Historical Recordings (DAHR), an online database, recording sessions for *Beggars of Life* were held in late August and early September at the Victor studio in Camden, New Jersey.

Over seven days, music was recorded for each of the film's nine reels by the Motion Picture Orchestra (a group of anonymous studio musicians). These recording sessions utilized an orchestra numbering 27, and once 34 men, and also featured a solo vocalist and a male quartet. Train sound effects were likewise recorded—though it's not known if these particular effects were used in the film, as the Victor studio records indicate they were dropped from later recording sessions. On August 23, a prologue was also recorded which featured a recitation by stage actor Harrison Brockbank. And on August 24, an epilogue was recorded. The nature of the prologue and epilogue is unknown, as well as whether either was used.

Other records that shed a little more light on the spoken dialogue heard in *Beggars of Life* include censorship records from the state of New York. Paramount Famous Lasky Corporation applied for a license to show the silent film in New York in early August. After being reviewed by state censors, the silent version was granted a license as "suitable for adults."

And then the sound version was released. In October, the state's Motion Picture Division requested a copy of the dialogue heard in the sound version. In return, they received a copy of a document titled "Song Sung by Wallace Beery in *Beggars of Life*," suggesting this was the extent of the dialogue in the film. That document is reproduced here.

SONG SUNG BY WALLACE BEERY IN "BEGGARS OF LIFE"

Verse 2: My girl is very fascinating,
          I don't believe it over-rating,
          In a back room of a bum saloon
          That's where she sits all day.
          I wonder where she sits at night,
          Hark those bells, Hark those bells
          (Train - whistles twice)
          That's where she sits all day,
          I wonder where she sits at night.

Verse 3: My girl is very fascinating,
          I don't believe it over-rating,
          In a back room of a bum saloon
          that's where she sits all day,
          I wonder where she sits at night,
          Hark those bells, Hark those bells
          (Beery's voice - ooh - ooh -)
          That's where she sits all day,
          I wonder where she sits at night.

Verse 1: My girl is very fascinating,
          I don't believe it over-rating,
          In a back room of a bum saloon
          That's where she sits all day,
          I wonder where she sits at night,
          Hark those bells, Hark those bells

          That's where she sits all day,
          I wonder where she sits at night.
          What a fine bunch of jungle buzzards
          you guys are.

In this Paramount publicity photo, Louise Brooks holds a
hobo sign indicating "Police hostile to tramps"

A SLICE OF AMERICANA

In more ways than one, *Beggars of Life* can be seen as a cinematic slice of Americana. And as such, there are stories behind the story of film and its making. These background bits and pieces include the train used in the movie, the film's connection with the great American pastime, baseball, and most importantly, the film's depiction of hobo life.

Locomotive 102

The uncredited star of *Beggars of Life* is Locomotive 102. That was the designation of the engine which not only transported the cast and crew on a daily basis, but was featured in some of the film's most dramatic scenes. In fact, this engine played three different trains in the movie. Wellman called it a "beautiful plaything."

The location work on *Beggars of Life* took place in and around the Carrizo Gorge, a rough stretch of railway some fifty miles to the east of Jacumba. The trains that road on this track belonged to the SD&A (San Diego & Arizona) Railway.

In 1919, SD&A took possession of two large Class C-31 2-8-0 locomotives (the latter numbers refer to the engine's wheel configuration) built by the American Locomotive Company in Schenectady, New York. They were numbered engines 101 and 102, and both went to work on the nearly 150 miles of track stretching from San Diego to points east, including Jacumba and further down the line, Yuma. Named the "Impossible Railroad" due to its rugged terrain, much of the track was cut through solid rock, with over two thirds of it traversing numerous curves, tunnels, and wooden trestles. These geographic features, as well as the engine designation, can be glimpsed in the film.

In May and June of 1928, Locomotive 102 was pressed into service during the making of *Beggars of Life*. In "On Location with Billy Wellman," Brooks affectionately remembered the train. The actress wrote, "We fell in love with Locomotive 102 on the first morning, when she gave two long and two short blasts on her steam whistle to call us to work.... When everyone was accounted for by the assistant director, and after a warning ring of her bell, away Locomotive 102 skipped—up the canyons on the hour's trip to Carrizo Gorge, the central point from which we operated." Brooks remembered climbing over the locomotive and its cars, including its cow catcher and engine cab, and its boxcars and caboose. "If work finished at sunset, she returned to town in a frolicking mood, with clanging bell and blasting whistle. If work finished at night, she coasted to town on the breeze, with all of us lying out on the flatcars, looking up at the stars shimmering in the black sky."

Brooks also recounted how Wellman worked the train and its engineer, not unlike herself or Richard Arlen or one of the other actors. "Under Billy's expert guidance, she learned numerous tricks of changing speed and direction, of starting and stopping, with perfect timing." The result were some of the most dramatic scenes in the film.

Locomotive 102, which Brooks said made her engineer, fireman, and brakeman proud, continue to serve on the SD&A for nearly 40 years. In 1953, with newer and more powerful trains on the horizon, the once mighty engine was scrapped.

Baseball

It's notable that not one but two members of the cast of *Beggars of Life* gained distinction playing professional baseball, while a third also played organized ball.

One of them was tall, athletic, Edgar Washington, who plays Black Mose in the film. Washington was discovered while pitching for the Los Angeles White Sox of the Negro League. "Rube" Foster (the father of Black baseball) spotted Washington during the Chicago American Giants' 1916 West Coast tour. Washington was invited to travel along and pitch for the legendary team, which would eventually produce three National Baseball Hall of Famers. During Washington's tenure with the American Giants, he pitched in seven games, recording three victories against one loss versus white aggregations of the Pacific Coast and Northwestern Leagues. "Ed Washington," as sports writers initially referred to him, made a name for himself as he ruled the mound with an unorthodox pitching style. In 1920, Washington joined the newly formed Kansas City Monarchs, where he started at first base and batted .275 in 24 games. After a few months of barnstorming, however, Washington left the Monarchs and returned to Los Angeles. That same year, after his first try at acting, Washington rejoined the Los Angeles White Sox for yet a few more games. Between gigs, Washington continued to play ball, and is believed to have occasionally played for Alexander's Giants in the integrated California Winter League. [Washington's son, Kenny Washington, was a two-sport great—the first African-American to play baseball at UCLA, the first Bruin to be named an All-American, and the first African-American to sign a contract with a National Football League team in the post-World War II era. His teammate, Jackie Robinson, described him as the greatest football player he had have ever seen.]

The other ball player in the cast of *Beggars of Life* was Mike Donlin, who plays a hobo. Donlin was a rowdy fellow known as "Turkey Mike," a nickname he received because of his unique gait as well as for his entertaining personality and flamboyant dress.

Donlin was an outfielder whose career ran from 1899 to 1914. He played for seven teams, most of them in the National League. Notably, he played for the New York Giants, where he starred in the outfield for John McGraw's 1904 pennant winner and 1905 World Series champion. (One NYC review of *Beggars of Life* mentioned Donlin by name and reminded readers of his past sporting prowess.)

Donlin was one of the finest hitters of the dead-ball era, and his .333 career batting average ranks 28th all time. He finished in the top three in batting five times, and in each of those same seasons, he also finished in the top ten in the league in on-base percentage, slugging percentage, and home runs. After he retired, Donlin moved to Hollywood, where friend and drinking buddy

John Barrymore helped him attain work.

Star Ball Player Takes Leading Role

Mike Donlin, whose acting fame threatens to overshadow his renown as a star baseball player with the New York Giants, has returned from a sanitarium to take the most important role of his career in Hollywood. He will have an important part in Paramount's film production of Jim Tully's "Beggars of Life." Wallace Beery dominates the story in the character of a hard fisted king of the hobos, while Louise Brooks and Richard Arlen have featured roles.

Another of the film's actors who played baseball was Guinn "Big Boy" Williams, the cart driver in *Beggars of Life*. Williams' father, a Texas politician who later served in Congress, secured his son an appointment to West Point after he returned home from the First World War, but Williams wasn't interested; instead, he decided to try his hand at baseball. The 6'2" athlete spent a brief time playing semi-pro ball in the American Southwest before heading to Hollywood.

In this Paramount publicity photo, Louise Brooks holds the
key to the "signs most generally used by tramps to
convey messages to their brethren."

The hobo key ...

1. Main street good for begging.
2. Rock pile in connection with jail.
3. Speakeasies in town.
4. Prohibition enforced in town.
5. Police are hostile. Look out.
6. Police not hostile to tramps.
7. Police hostile to tramps.
8. Leaving railroad for highway or across country.
9. Railroad police not hostile.
10. Railroad police hostile.
11. Used in connection with any other sign means next town.
12. Church or religious people. Use religion game for begging.
13. Town is hostile. Get out quick.
14. Main street N.G.
15. Good people live here.
16. Cranky woman or bad dog.
17. People do not give.
18. Bad man lives here.
19. Negro section good for hobos.
20. Cooties in jail.
21. Good clean jail.
22. Jail clean but prisoners starve.
23. Jail filthy.
24. City detectives are in plain clothes.
25. Workhouse in connection with jail.
26. Waiting in town for person named.
27. Name and direction of travel.
28. Circle town.
29. Jail good for night's lodging.

Hobo Life

At the time of its release, much was made of the hobo subculture which underpins *Beggars of Life*. Paramount called the film an "epic of Hobohemia," claiming it was the "first important picture depicting the lives of America's half-million homeless wanderers." True or not—the publicity department soon reduced the number to 50,000—*Beggars of Life* was for many a first glimpse of a little seen way of life.

To introduce the public to this "unusual milieu," Paramount's publicity department issued a series of articles and photographs explaining the habits, lives, and motives of "hoboland." One hyperbolic piece, titled "Secrets of Hobohemia Torn Open in Picture" stated, "Here is the picture to tap the vein of wanderlust in every man; a picture in tune with the changing times. Here is a picture of picturesque fellows with romance in their eyes, kicked, cuffed, beaten, hounded but finding adventure at every turn. Here is a picture of those strange anti-social beings, living without the law, wandering, drifting around, beggars of life."

Other pieces, like "German Women Kindest, Veteran Tramps Decide" and "Childlike Faith Leads Wanderers" were just as fanciful. Only "Hobohemia Hides Hundreds of Hunted Men, Allan Pinkerton, Famous Detective, Says" suggested a darker side to life on the road.

The closest publicity materials or the film itself came to depicting actual hobo subculture was in its use of language, and that it did sparingly. "There are many strange jargons and lingoes in tramp life," Tully was quoted in the Paramount Press Sheet. "Tramps are inventors of words for their own use which now and then pass into popular slang and sometimes into the language."

Among the words mentioned in the Press Sheet were "gay-cat" (a tenderfoot in Hobodom), "chuck-a-dummy" (to feign a faint in order to gain sympathy), "California blankets" (newspapers used to sleep on), and "flipping" (train riding). However, only a few tramp terms, such as "jungle" (a meeting place for hoboes), "jungle buzzards" (lesser hoboes), and "Bo" (used to address someone in a familiar way) are found in the film's inter-titles.

Despite such touches, as well as the hobo graffiti scratched onto the wooden walls of a boxcar, the film's authenticity was called into question, especially by the Tully faithful.

Martin Dickstein, writing in the *Brooklyn Daily Eagle*, went so far as to state, "The unwary filmgoer is warned that if he wanders into the Paramount Theater this week expecting to see an accurate movie version of Jim Tully's *Beggars of Life* he will be doomed to bitterest disappointment—if not downright consternation. For, if the truth must be known, the only recognizable portion of that originally glorious narrative of hobo life which has been retained in the celluloid edition is the title. It's a subject for wonder why even this has been permitted to remain intact. *Jungle Passion*, or something equally incandescent—and silly—would have been a more appropriate label. The movies have made *Beggars of Life* into something as clean and harmless as Mary's little lamb."

Other newspaper and magazine critics, some of whom seemed to have read Tully's book, thought the film didn't stick closely enough to the original text. *Film Mercury* commented, "Those who are Jim Tully 'fans' will consider the production not quite as vital as the literary works of the author. Others may think it too realistic for the cinema."

The Saga of the Hobo

Wallace Beery will relive many of his own experiences in "Beggars of Life," a story of "the road."

By Myrtle Gebhart

Wally Beery hopes "Beggars of Life" will be a success, so he will have an opportunity to play more rôles of the same type.

IN the Texas twilight, which isn't twilight at all, but a misty, slate-gray envelope of gloom, two kids sat by a water tank, just outside the town of Gainsborough, and jawed. It was odd, the uncommon lot of things they found to talk about, when there was no life stirring in all that stretch—either way. In the fraternizing of the road, community of interest usually ends with such matters as food and cops.

But "Red" had found the arrow on the tank—the direction of a pal who had preceded him West. "The Fox" had made a pretense of combing the shock of matted hair above his rough-hewn, big-boned face. Wearied by such effort, they had appraised each other and decided upon confidence—guardedly.

"They're gettin' horstile down here," Red observed. "Never saw them Dallas dicks stir their dogs so much before." His chuckle carried a note of appreciative memory. "I'm headed for the Coast. Some day I'm goin' to write books." His eyes indicated that sarcasm would be resented.

"Yeah?" The Fox shifted a leg, stretched, and said: "You and I got ambition, 'bo. I'm goin' to be an actor, wear swell, silk tights, and play Rom-co. No more moochin' for me."

Just two bums, about twenty-two years ago, dreaming dreams. Their keen ears picked up a distant rumble, and, as it sang down to them along the shining rails, they ambled into a thicket. When the train had picked up its speed again, Jim Tully and Edwin Carewe slept contentedly on the rods, despite the sand and stone that was blown, like hail, against their faces.

About the same time, a roughneck, overgrown boy, with a widespread grin over his spatulate features, swung with the lurch of the speeding express. He was riding, as an experienced bum should, the blind baggage. His bulk did not fit well in the lower berths used by the more slim and wiry 'bos. Soon, when his vehicle slowed into the yards, he would make his way to an outgoing freight and into a cattle car, unmindful of the stench that was blown in his face.

They called him "Jumbo," because of his elephantine hugeness, and those big hands—like hams—that slapped the pachyderms such resounding smacks.

At present, he was making the best of an experience common to all nomads of the little, gyp circuses. He

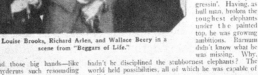

Louise Brooks, Richard Arlen, and Wallace Beery in a scene from—"Beggars of Life."

had been "red-lighted" (thrown off the pay roll for a minor offense), and forbidden to come on the grounds. In that way they wouldn't have to pay him his dollar fifty a week "hold-back" at the end of the season. Three and a half a week, and a dollar fifty hold-back, if you got it, had looked grand to him a few months before. So had the scuffed brogans that had hardly any soles left now. All his life he'd never had new clothes of his own, nothing but hand-me-downs, until the brogans.

But he was progressing. Having, as bull man, broken the toughest elephants under the painted top, he was growing ambitious. Barnum didn't know what he was missing. Why, hadn't he disciplined the stubbornest elephants? The world held possibilities, all of which he was capable of realizing.

If anybody had told Jumbo Beery, nineteen and carefree, that he would some day be an actor, that he would

The Saga of the Hobo

Louise Brooks has the rôle of a girl who evades the law by donning boy's clothes and mingling with hobos.

three years he was with the circus, and for two years, —just bumming. He wore the black satine "thousand-mile" shirt, the bothersome washing of which could be postponed indefinitely. He sat down to "mulligan" with many a likewise begrimed, but happy, confrère of the rails in many a moonlit "jungle" in the woods— the rendezvous of the leisurely gents. Many a back door was slammed in his face, but not every housewife could resist his bland humor.

"Couldn't get away with the pathetic stuff. So I always asked, just to be polite, if there was any wood they wanted cut, but I explained I'd cut my thumb at the last place, or sprained my wrist, and if they didn't insist on my taking off the dirty bandage so they could see, I'd get my 'lump.'" "Lump" being, in the elegant parlance of the 'bo, a handout. "Or else I'd have some jokes on tap, and get 'em laughing.

"Sure," he replied to my observation, "you work harder as a hobo than you do earning an honest living. You've got to use your brains."

Curious how interesting it is to find out how the other half lives. A hobo, to me, has always been a very soiled individual to whom you gingerly held out sandwiches. That there could be castes—a social and ethical system—among them, and dreams, talents and ambitions, was one of the surprises Beery and Tully handed me, along with memories of their bumming days, and words which my typewriter has not been trained to record. A lady of delicate sensibilities is instantly shocked at their language. I was shocked. But it had this to its credit; it was *different*.

"There are classes of hobos," they explained. "The road kid, in search of adventure, is usually out only a few months. He gets his fill and goes home. Fellows get tired of sedentary life, and want a thrill. Another gets strapped, and has to ride the rods home to the wife and kids. Those are the transients. The seasoned 'bo just has the wanderlust. He can't stand the monotony of steady work. He is visionary, and a dreamer. The yegg is the aristocrat. He robs country banks and always has money; he rides at the company's expense, because it's against his principles to pay railroad fare. He swaggers around the 'jungle' and often brings the makin's for a 'set-down' (a regular meal) and the treats.

"Hobos are mostly Irish. There are no Jews. Few who have been on the mooch for a couple of years ever settle down to commonplace life. Jack Lon-

live in a mansion, be waited on and have a beautiful wife, his hearty guffaw would have rumbled down the length of cars, and shaken the scared schoolmar'm out of her berth. Such thoughts never entered his head.

Years later, two men in ragged shirts and nondescript pants swung onto the rods of a freight on a siding, under the California sunshine. They were Red and Jumbo. The water tank was there, and the atmosphere seemed right. But there were cameras and mirrors reflecting the light, and the two men had grown heavier and older. They were filming "Beggars of Life," which stars Wallace Beery. It is the saga of the hobo.

"The kangaroo court" is the hobo tribunal which meets in the woods, and "tries" members of its fraternity according to their own code.

At nineteen Wally Beery bade the family a nonchalant farewell, unmindful of his Irish dad's storming, but embarrassed by his Swiss mother's rare outburst of tears, and got a job with a circus. His first week's wages paid for a pair of brogans.

For five years he ridiculed steady employment. For

don was on the road. Jack Dempsey, 'Kid' McCoy, and Stanley Ketchell were road kids. Many of them become pugilists. William Wellman, who is directing 'Beggars of Life,' was a road kid, beating his way to the lumber camps. For five years, intermittently, James Cruze was on the bum. He would connect with a theater

Continued on page 109

The Saga of the Hobo

Continued from page 59

job—grip, usher, super—and, when he got fired, move on to some other small town with a stock company, via the beams. A lot of great men probably were hobos, if they would admit it."

Self-pity is the first thing the road takes away from you. If you aren't a weakling, and crushed, you learn to fight.

"Fearlessness, the primitive fundamentals, human nature, and with these the road teaches you," Beery said. "You have nerve—but no nerves."

"The intelligence of many of the several hundred thousand hobos of America would surprise the citified 'reformer,'" Tully broke in. "Oddly the 'bo is at once a cynic—stripped of illusion, he has no chance to develop ideals—and a blind dreamer. Many of them make for the libraries the minute they hit a town. After seven years in an orphanage in Ohio, I hit the road, an untrained, scared, and miserable kid. Soon I was as hard as nails. But another kid, somewhere, took me to a library with him, and I began to read. I'd write doggerel on scraps of brown paper, and when I was still in my teens I had read Balzac, Dumas, and classics that the cute college lads never learn.

"Of course, the life wasn't *perfect*. You were hungry sometimes. And there were the dicks. They'd round you up, along with the other vags, and try to pin on you everything that had happened in the State of Kansas —or Illinois or Ohio—in the last five years. What chance had a 'bo of proving an alibi, when he had no last name, and only a 'nick' for a front name?"

In his customary way, Wally does things with gusto. First, his heavy, steady tramp, that threatens to shake the building. His thunderous laugh. He is louder, broader, merrier, than the equally huge, but more gentle, Noah.

The story of "Beggars of Life," as it has been changed to meet movie requirements, concerns the adventures of a swashbuckling yegg, the high-class gent of the beams. *Oklahom Red* is his moniker, and he is modeled after a pal of the author's. Only—there's a love story here, and love is something that the cynical soul of the 'bo does not know. Loyalty, generosity, and other fine qualities he comes in contact with, but the right kind of a girl he never meets, except in those books in the libraries.

The movies, however, are elastic. There is a girl in this hobo's life. Just out of an orphanage, the heavy hand of the law grasps her for a crime she believes she has committed. She is aided to escape by a road kid. Dressed in boy's clothes, she accompanies him. Louise Brooks plays the girl tramp, Richard Arlen the kid. They are found and taken into the jungle before the "kangaroo court," where the lawless gents, who have their own code, are given mock trials. The swaggering, big brute of a yegg, *Oklahoma Red*, sits as judge. The kid's fright provides great amusement, as he is tried for being a sissy. *Oklahoma Red* awards himself the custody of the girl—of course, the blustering *Red* does the noble self-sacrificing act. A wow of a rôle, it would seem, for Wally, and those who complain of the ornate unreality of most movies won't be annoyed by gorgeous settings in this one.

While we talked, Wally outlined another rôle he would like.

" 'The Bull Man!' Get that title? He breaks elephants. Cruel. Strong. Girl—snappy little Clara Bow temper—falls for him. Wants to be an elephant trainer. He teaches her. He thinks he can crush her spirit. *She* breaks him—he turns yellow—she's in danger, the bull turns on her —he pulls himself together, rescues her—egoism."

The ease of effete civilization has not made Beery soft. He is still, in many ways, Jumbo. His humor is broad slapstick at times. Yet it is not without subtlety. Recently he carried a new mutt dog around the studio, to acquaint it with picture making, in order that it might hold its conversational own in bow-wows with Hollywood canines. Poking into an office, where a conference between executives was in progress, he surveyed the scene solemnly, said to the dog: "Now, you know what a conference is," and slammed the door.

Style is a word not in his vocabulary, though the lovely chatelaine of his home speaks it beautifully. During the filming of "Old Ironsides," when a fleet of sleek yachts skimmed over the Catalina waters, outside camera range, he rigged up a boat with a pop-gun motor, apparently made of tin cans held together by strings, and sailed proudly among them. When he can "take off" the grandeur that is Hollywood, he is in his element.

Yet his heart is big, beneath his gruffness. Many a hungry kid has been helped by his bounty. His parents, seventy-odd years old, now enjoy, in California, a comfort they never dreamed of realizing.

88

Any adaption of a literary work is tricky, and sometimes unsatisfactory. It was a dilemma William Wellman and Benjamin Glazer and others involved in the making of the film might not have been able to solve.

In their superb biography of Tully, authors Paul Bauer and Mark Dawidziak note that scholar Nels Anderson, author of the pioneering study *The Hobo: The Sociology of the Homeless Man* (1923), lavished praise on Tully's 1924 book in one of its first reviews. At the time, Anderson stated, "Besides being a faithful picture of the road, *Beggars of Life* is an excellent display of hobo slang, morals, ethics, and above all, the philosophy of the underworld. In this respect Tully has not been excelled." It was high praise, and it created high expectations.

In 1928, Anderson previewed the film for Paramount, and wrote Tully that Hollywood's disdain for reality had marred the resulting movie, especially in regard to its depiction of hobo life. Nevertheless, Anderson concluded, "the film was historically significant in capturing the rural hobo before city life and the automobile moved him from the tracks back to the highway, where he had been before the railroads."

"BEGGARS OF LIFE"
With Wallace Beery, Louise Brooks, Richard Arlen. William Wellman Production, from Jim Tully's saga of Hobohemia.

PARAMOUNT

90

CREDITS

Studio: Paramount Famous Lasky Corp.
Producer: Adolph Zukor and Jesse L. Lasky
General Manager: B.P. Shulberg
Director: William A. Wellman
Assistant Director: Charles Barton and Otto Brower
Unit Manager: R.L. Johnston and Frank Newman Jr.
Casting Director: Fred Datig
Writing Credits: Benjamin Glazer and Jim Tully
   (screenplay, with uncredited contributions by
   Maxwell Anderson, Myron M. Stearns, Harry Behn);
   adapted from the book by Jim Tully; titles by Julian
   Johnson
Script Supervisor: Margery Chapin Wellman
Script Clerks: Ann Bergman, Helen Cavender
Art Direction: Hans Dreier
Cinematography: Henry Gerrard
Second Cameraman: Guy Bennett
Assistant Cameraman: Cliff Shirpser and Bob Rhea
Film Editor: Alyson Schaffer
Recording Director (Movietone): Roy Pomeroy
Sound Editors: Andy Newman, Merrill White
Foley Recordist: Benjamin Glazer
Costumes: Travis Banton, with Edith Head
Makeup: James Collins
Property Man: John Richmond
Grip: Mitch Crawley
Assistant Grip: Andy Durkins

Stuntmen: Matt Gilman – Wallace Beery double; Duke
   Green – stuntman; Jack Holbrook – Richard Arlen
   double; Harvey Parry – Louise Brooks double

Production work on the film took place between May
18 and June 18, 1928, with location shooting near
Jacumba, California taking place between May 30 and
June 15. The film was released in both a silent and sound
version; the sound version included music, sound effects,
a bit of dialogue, and a song reportedly sung by Wallace
Beery.

Beggars of Life was officially released September 22,
1928 (elsewhere reported as September 15), with a length
of 9 reels (reported as 7,504 and 7,560 feet), and a
running time of 80 and 87 minutes. The sound version of
the film premiered at the Paramount theater in New York
City on September 18, with noted band leader Paul Ash
performing on stage prior to the film. (An advertisement
for the premiere is pictured at the beginning of this
chapter.) Earlier showings of the silent version took place
in Indianapolis, Indiana and Salt Lake City, Utah
beginning on September 1, in Battle Creek, Michigan
beginning on September 2, and elsewhere.

Under its American title, documented screenings of
the film took place in Australia, Canada, China, France,
India, Ireland, Jamaica, Japan, New Zealand, South
Africa, Sweden, and the United Kingdom (England, Isle
of Man, and Scotland).

Elsewhere, *Beggars of Life* is known to have been shown
under the title *Les mendiants de la vie* (Algeria); *Bettler des
Lebens* (Austria); *Meias indiscretag* and *Mendigos da vida*
(Brazil); *Mendigos de la Vida* (Chile); *Žebráci života*
and *Žebráky živote* (Czechoslovakia); *De Lovløses Tog*
(Denmark); *Menschen Zijn Nooit Tevreden* (Dutch East

Indies - Indonesia); *Les mendiants de la vie* (France); *Az orszagutak angyala* (Hungary); *I mendicanti della vita* (Italy); *Bettler des Lebens* and *Dzives ubagi* (Latvia); *Bettlers des Lebens (Les Mendiants de la Vie)* (Luxembourg); *Mendigos de vida* (Mexico); *Menschen Zijn Nooit Tevreden* and *Zwervers* (The Netherlands); *Ludzie bezdomni* (Poland); *Mendigos da vida* (Portugal); *Strada cersetorilor* (Romania); *Captaires de vida* and *Mendigos de vida* (Spain); *Les mendiants de la vie* (Switzerland).

Beggars of Life was popular in Paris in late 1929 and early 1930, where it played at the same time as another popular Louise Brooks' film, *Diary of a Lost Girl*

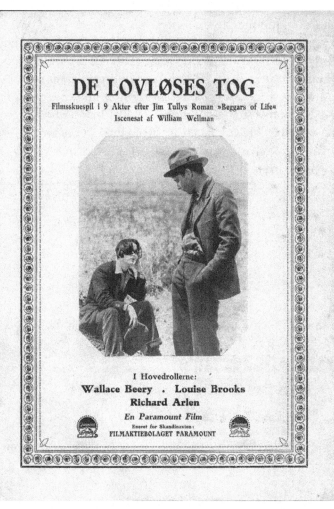

The cover of a Danish program

Beggars of Life was shown around Asia, including Japan

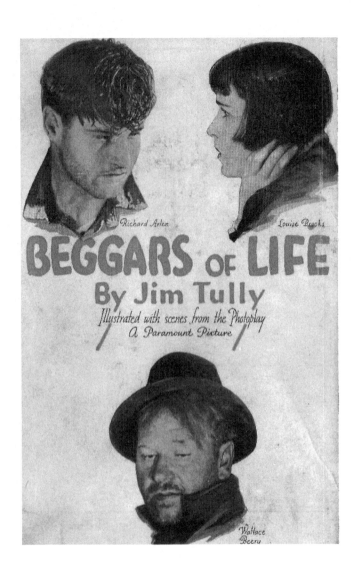

Cover of the American photoplay edition,
issued by Grosset & Dunlap

LEARN MORE

Beggars of Life was widely written about when first released. Articles appeared in newspapers, trade publications and fan magazines including *National Board of Review Magazine*, Sept. 1928; *The Bioscope*, Sept. 12, 1928; *Kinematograph Weekly*, Sept. 13, 1928; *Variety*, Sept. 26, 1928; *Motion Picture News*, Sept. 26, 1928; *Musical Courier*, Sept. 27, 1928; *Weekly Film Review*, Sept. 29, 1928; *Harrison's Reports*, Sept. 29, 1928; *Billboard*, Sept. 29, 1928; *Film Daily*, Sept. 30, 1928; *Film Mercury*, Oct. 5, 1928; *Detroit Saturday Night*, October 20, 1928; *Exhibitors Herald and Moving Picture World*, Oct. 20, 1928; *Film Spectator*, Oct. 27, 1928; *Hollywood Filmograph*, Oct. 27, 1928; *Movie Makers*, Nov. 1928; *Picture-Play*, Nov. 1928; *Educational Screen*, Jan. 1929; *Motion Picture*, Jan. 1929; *Picture-Play*, Jan. 1929; *Picturegoer*, June 1929; *Picture Show*, June 20, 1929.

A more comprehensive bibliography, including magazine and newspaper citations from around the world, can be found on the Louise Brooks Society website.

The following annotated checklist of books and films will help place the film in context.

Tully, Jim. *Beggars of Life*. New York: A. & C. Boni, 1924. — literary source for the film; reissued by AK Press/ Nabat in 2004, and Kent State University Press in 2010

Tully, Jim. *Beggars of Life: Illustrated with Scenes from the Photoplay, a Paramount Picture*. New York: Grosset & Dunlap, 1928.
— the Tully book with added scene stills from the film. A photoplay edition was also issued in the UK by Wm Collins Sons & Co. with a different cover and no additional illustrations (see following illustration)

Brownlow, Kevin. *The Parade's Gone By*. New York: Alfred A. Knopf, 1968.
— includes interviews with Wellman and Brooks

Wellman, William A. *A Short Time for Insanity: An Autobiography*. New York: Hawthorn Books, 1974.
— autobiography of the director

Brooks, Louise. *Lulu in Hollywood*. New York: Knopf, 1982.
— includes "On Location with Billy Wellman" and other essays which touch on Brooks' film work

Thompson, Frank T. *William A. Wellman*. Metuchen, New Jersey: Scarecrow Press, 1983.
— contains four pages on the film and other references

Vermilye, Jerry. *The Films of the Twenties*. Secaucus, New Jersey: Citadel Press, 1985.
— includes a brief chapter on the film

Ventura, Claude. *Jacumba Hôtel*. 1985.
— French television documentary about the making of *Beggars of Life*, with commentary by Philippe Garnier

Hinkle, Ray. *The Hobo from St. Marys: A Tribute to Jim Tully.* St. Marys, Ohio: Ray Hinkle, 1986.
— 85-page self-published booklet

Paris, Barry. *Louise Brooks.* New York: Knopf, 1989.
— biography of the actress, with discussion of the film

Robinson, Todd. *Wild Bill: Hollywood Maverick—The Life and Times of William A. Wellman.* Wild Bill Pictures, 1996.
— documentary of the filmmaker

Wellman, Jr., William. *The Man and His Wings.* West Port, Connecticut: Praeger, 2006.
— includes a brief discussion of the film

Bauer, Paul, and Mark Dawidziak. *Jim Tully: American Writer, Irish Rover, Hollywood Brawler.* Kent, Ohio: Kent State University Press, 2011.
— biography of the author, with discussion of the film

Dixon, Bryony. *100 Silent Films.* London: British Film Institute, 2011.
— includes a brief chapter on the film

Stone, Mark Wade. *Road Kid to Writer.* StoryWorks.TV, 2011.
— 50 minute documentary based on the 2011 Tully biography

Wellman, Jr., William. *Wild Bill Wellman: Hollywood Rebel.* New York: Pantheon Books, 2015.
— includes extensive discussion of the film

Donnelly, K. J., and Ann-Kristin Wallengren. *Today's Sounds for Yesterday's Films: Making Music for Silent Cinema.* New York, NY: Palgrave Macmillan, 2016.
— discussion of the film and its music by Michael Hammond, a member of the Dodge Brothers

Wellman, William. *Beggars of Life.* Kino Lorber, 2017.
— best available DVD / Blu-ray release , with audio commentaries by William Wellman Jr. and Thomas Gladysz and a musical score by the Mont Alto Motion Picture Orchestra

Gallagher, John Andrew and Frank Thompson. *Nothing Sacred: The Cinema of William Wellman.* Men With Wings Press, 2017.
— a comprehensive study of Wellman's film work

British photoplay edition, issued by Wm Collins Sons & Co.

Those interested in finding out more about *Beggars of Life* should check out the Louise Brooks Society website at www.pandorasbox.com. A website devoted to Jim Tully seems to be no longer available, though a search will turn up many worthwhile results.

Also worth checking out are the websites for the Mont Alto Motion Picture Orchestra at www.mont-alto.com as well as The Dodge Brothers at www.dodgebrothers.co.uk

SHE'S A DREAM

RICHARD ARLEN—LOUISE BROOKS IN THE WILLIAM A.WELLMAN PRODUCTION
"BEGGARS OF LIFE" A PARAMOUNT PICTURE
Two-column Production Mat 2P—.10

FOR weeks they fled through the mazes of Hobohemia, a boy searching for the Golden Fleece, a girl caught in the whirlpool of life. Into the haunts of the homeless, braving the unknown and the danger. Until they awaken to love.

ABOUT THE AUTHOR

Thomas Gladysz is the Director of the Louise Brooks Society (www.pandorasbox.com), which he founded in 1995. Gladysz has authored numerous articles on Brooks and early film, and has contributed program notes to the San Francisco Silent Film Festival, Telluride Film Festival, Syracuse CineFest, EbertFest, University of Wisconsin Cinematheque, and others. In 2010, he edited and wrote the introduction to the Louise Brooks edition of *The Diary of a Lost Girl*, the book that was the basis for the 1929 film. In 2017, Gladysz compiled *Now We're in the Air – The Story*, after assisting in a small way with the restoration of the once lost Brooks' film. His audio commentaries can be heard on two Kino Lorber DVD / Blu-rays, *Beggars of Life* and *Diary of a Lost Girl*. Gladysz has lectured and organized exhibits on the actress at the San Francisco Public Library, and introduced her films at the Castro Theater, Niles Essanay Silent Film Museum, Detroit Institute of Arts, and Action Cinema in Paris, France.

Gladysz continues to research Louise Brooks, and blogs about the actress on a regular basis while listening to his online radio station devoted to the actress & the silent era, RadioLulu, which includes music associated with *Beggars of Life*.